AUNT JO's
INDIA

WRITTEN AND ILLUSTRATED BY

Sona and Jacob

APPLE BOOKS®

Hello! I am Jo! You can call me Aunt Jo! So does everybody... Let me be your travel guide today and let us explore the truly magical land of India. The birthplace of one of the earliest civilisations, India is steeped in culture, history, mystique... a vibrant place with so many languages and communities, so many different types of people... So boot up and let's go exploring... all across India!

Meet Professor Janus. He is a very clever scientist who knows almost every thing about any thing. So if we need to clarify something, we can always ask him…

Where is India? India is situated in the **southern part of Asia.** The land forms a **peninsula -** covered on three sides by water and one side by land. The Bay of Bengal on the east, the Arabian Sea on the west and the Indian Ocean in the south surround it.

The total area is about **3,287,590 sq. km.** With a population of over 1 billion people, India is the second-highest populated country in the world.

India is truly a diverse land. With over **14 major** and more than **1,000 minor** languages and dialects, Indians - Hindus and Muslims, Christians and Sikhs, Parsis and Jains and Buddhists… co-exist peacefully… India is full of broad plains, mighty rivers, the world's tallest mountain system and tropical lowlands…

The people of the Indus valley planned their cities very carefully. Building many of their buildings on mud platforms, their houses were made of baked or sun-dried bricks. The houses were so well-planned and the people had such a sense of social living and hygiene that most homes had a bathing area that was supplied with water from a nearby public well or from a well in the courtyard of the house.

The Indus Valley... the beginning of a great civilisation!

Did you know that the name **'India'** came from the **River Indus,** the valleys around which were the home of the early settlers? Over 4,500 years ago, several farming and herding communities, came together and set up a trading system in the northwestern part of India. Over time, this group of people, laid out carefully planned cities and formed the Indus Valley Civilisation!

Professor Janus says that the Indus people traded very extensively, with nearby agricultural communities and with distant mining areas. Goods traded included cotton, timber, grain and livestock. For transport, people used pack animals, riverboats and ox carts.

Though scholars have been unable to decipher them, perhaps the most interesting objects found at the Indus valley sites, are square stone seals with pictographs and drawings of animals.

The Indus Valley people were also great artisans. They used copper and bronze to make tools, mirrors, pots, and pans. Bone, shell, and ivory were used to create ornaments, tools, game pieces, and inlay for furniture. Indus artisans also crafted silver and gold utensils and ornaments, as well as ornaments made of stoneware and earthenware.

The wonders of ancient India

Ancient India was a vibrant land with knowledge galore! Not only were early Indians the masters of shipbuilding and architecture, they were also the pioneers of mathematical theorems and formulae, astronomical ideas and theories, medical breakthroughs and architectural expertise...

The **number system** as we know it today was first invented in India. In fact, it was Aryabhatta who put forward the concept of a zero and explained how the digit worked. And in about the 5th Century A.D., Bhaskaracharya rightly calculated the time taken by the earth to orbit the sun - 365.258756484 days.

A sage named Boddhidharma took the art of **Kalaripayat** from Kerala to China in the 5th century A.D. The Chinese called him Po-ti-tama. He taught this art in a temple. This temple is today known as the Shaolin temple. Thus Judo, Karate, Kung Fu and other similar martial arts, which are today identified with the Far East, actually originated from India.

The ancient Indian language of **Sanskrit,** taught and learned even today, is considered the most precise language in terms of construct and grammar and therefore the best suited language for computer software.

Did you know that the world's **first university** was established in Takshila in 700 B.C.? More than 10,500 students from all over the world studied more than 60 subjects. The University of Nalanda built in the 4th century A.D. was one of the greatest achievements of ancient India in the field of education.

The earliest school of medicine known to mankind was **Ayurveda!** Charaka - the father of Indian medicine - consolidated this complete system about 2,500 years ago!

The Kings of India

The first great emperor of India was **Chandragupta Maurya,** who founded the Maurya Empire and ruled from about 321 to 298 B.C. He was a very just king, who instituted strict punishments, while providing great benefits for his people.

Ashoka the Great, Chandragupta's grandson, expanded his grandfather's kingdom so much that the Maurya empire extended far into south India during his time. He fought many a war, including the historical battle of Kalinga, where the bloodshed touched him and he gave up war. He preached and sent out emissaries of Buddhism,all across the land and into Sri Lanka and the Far East.

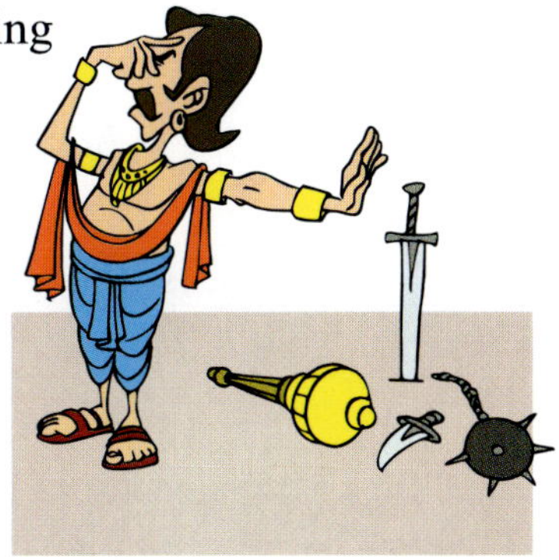

The Kushanas invaded India in 100 A.D. and set up a mighty empire under **King Kanishka.** Kanishka's empire extended from Sin kiang (in what is now Chinese Turkestan) to Varanasi in eastern India.

The last of the great Kings was **Harsha,** who reigned from 606 A.D. to 647 A.D. He was the lord over the rulers of the Punjab, Kashmir, Nepal, and central India. However, unlike the Guptas, Harsha was not able to extend his power to southern India, which was ruled at that time by three powerful dynasties, the Pallavas, Pandyas and Cholas.

In the 350 A.D., another great King - **Samudragupta** - a scion of the Gupta Dynasty ruled India. He extended the Gupta Empire from northern India to the far south. One of the inscriptions set up in his reign mentions that he had conquered no fewer than 13 princes of the south. Samudragupta's reign is referred to as the **Golden Age** of the Guptas,

Invaders down the ages

The first invaders into India were the **Aryans,** from Central Asia and Persia in about 1500 BC. The Aryans spoke Sanskrit, ancient Iranian, Greek and Latin. The Aryans formulated the four major religious texts - the Vedas, which form the basis of Hindu religion and philosophy!

Heard of **Alexander the Great?** This Greek conqueror invaded India in 326 B.C. He fought many an Indian warrior on the banks of the Jhelum. In fact, his victory over Porus or Purushottam and his subsequent release of the King are a legend even today!

The Turks invaded India in the early 1000 A.D.'s. Between 1000 and 1030, **Mahmud of Ghazni** led a series of devastating raids into India. He was a soldier of remarkable ability and looted gold and silver from across the various Indian kingdoms. When he died in 1030 A.D., he left a kingdom in the Punjab, but the rest of India remained independent of Muslim rule.

The first Mughal conqueror was **Babar**. In 1526 Babar, a descendant of Tamerlane, invaded India from Kabul, Afghanistan, and defeat-ed Ibrahim Lodi, the Delhi sultan, at Panipat. He was such a skilful general that within a few years he had conquered most of northern India.

In 1192, another Turkish ruler of Afghanistan, **Muhammad of Ghor,** invaded Punjab and appointed a Turkish slave leader, Qutb al-Din Aybak, to be viceroy in Delhi. Between 1200 and 1210 Aybak consolidated Muslim conquests in India. He founded an empire, now known as the Delhi Sultanate. He commemorated his victories with a column 78 metres high - the **Qutb Minar.**

The **Guptas** ruled India from 320 to 500 A.D.. The Gupta period is considered India's golden age. Literature, sculpture and other arts reached a peak never attained again in India. Gupta wall paintings included vivid scenes of Indian life and events in Buddha's life. Most of the paintings that remain are in caves, such as at Ajanta.

Dynasties that ruled India

The **Maurya** emperors ruled from about 324 to 185 B.C. The Mauryas established a system of public irrigation works that helped farmers produce rich harvests. Craftsmen were encouraged and made cloth, gold, jewellery and wood products. The Maurya Empire traded with Greece, Malaya, Mesopotamia and Persia. Under the guidance of Ashoka, several architectural wonders were created, one of which, the four headed lion, is the symbol of India, today!

The **Cholas** were the most powerful empire in Southern India for more than 200 years. From 900 A.D. the Cholas, with their capital at Thanjavur, expanded their empire and took it up to Sri Lanka in the South. The Cholas are acknowledged for their architecture and metal work. In fact, the world's first granite temple, the Brihadeswara temple at Thanjavur was completed during the reign of Rajaraja Chola.

Did you know that a **"slave dynasty"** ruled India for more than 300 years? When Muhammed of Ghor seized much of India, he established his slave Qutb al-Din Aybak, to be viceroy in Delhi. Aybak and his heirs ruled India from 1206 to 1526 and were the "slave dynasty?

The **Mughals** ruled India from 1526 to 1857 A.D. They set up a system of centralised government. The Mughals were not only great Kings, but also great builders.

Mughal architecture is among India's most precious architecture today. The plan and construct of most buildings, including the Taj Mahal is awe-inspiring. It is believed that 20,000 craftsmen worked on the Taj for 22 years.

The first Mughal Emperor Babar, came to India and set up the Mughal Empire. The ferocious general that he was, he had conquered a good part of northern India in a few years. Babar was succeeded by his son Humayun, who was succeeded by Akbar the Great. Akbar is remembered as the greatest of the Great Mughal emperors. He was a born leader, a ferocious and feared soldier and he encouraged the arts and crafts...

The Mughals and their architecture

The Mughals who ruled India for a long period of time, consolidated their presence across the entire subcontinent, building beautiful monuments and palaces...

It was under Akbar's rule that the famous Fatehpur Sikri was constructed. He wanted to build this capital to commemorate his victories and mark the birth of his first son, but the fact that he could not bring water to the dry land, made him abandon the idea. The architectural marvel - a beautiful medley of Islamic and Hindu architecture stands even today!

Akbar was succeeded by Jahangir, who was succeeded by Shah Jahan. Shah Jahan married the beautiful Mumtaz Mahal, who died while giving birth to his fourteenth child. To mark his love for his queen, Shah Jahan built the **Taj Mahal.** Made of pure white marble brought from Iran, this architectural masterpiece was studded with precious stones... Today it houses the tombs of Shah Jahan and his beloved Mumtaz...

Shah Jahan was succeed by his son Aurangazeb. Aurangazeb's rule was the longest among the Mughal Kings. The Mughals spawned a glorious culture, which gave rise to beautiful musical styles, dance forms, food, crafts and much more...

Europeans in India

The reports of India's riches soon reached the Middle East and then Europe... Everybody wanted spices from India... ivory, silk, coconuts, pepper... It was not long before, several European kings sent out their emissaries and their ships to establish trade contacts with India.

It was in 1497 that the Portuguese King Manuel I sent the navigator **Vasco da Gama** to find a sea route to India via the Cape of Good Hope. Do you know where that is? It is the southern tip of Africa! Da Gama reached the port of Calicut in 1498, and his fleet returned to Lisbon in 1499. The news of the Portuguese success in crossing the Indian Ocean and reaching the richest spice port in India caused alarm bells to ring in Italy.

The Portuguese ruled supreme for almost a century, trading extensively. After the Portuguese, it was the Dutch who rose to power. They set up settlements in Nagapattinam in Tamil Nadu and Cinsura in Bengal. They also set up the **Dutch East India Company.**

The **British East India Company** was founded in 1600. In the beginning the Company did not engage in any wars of expansion, but set up operations in three independent sovereign settlements in India, Madras (now Chennai), Bombay (now Mumbai), and Calcutta, and each grew into substantial trading ports. Did you know that the ports were all fortified with sea walls and cannon?

What was the French angle to the whole thing? The French government granted a charter to the **French East India Company** in the 1720's. The French made their headquarters at Pondicherry in southern India and within 20 years or so the French had become so powerful that they were competing successfully with the British. The commercial rivalry soon took on political overtones and the military conflicts that resulted saw the British winning by a mile, thereby establishing their supremacy in India.

The British in India

1757 is considered to be the year when the **British Empire started in India.** Though it did take the British another 100 years to expand their control to the northern and western parts of India, 1757 marked the beginning of a rule that would last almost 200 years, giving rise to one of the most famous freedom struggles ever seen in the world.

The British formed a system where a Governor General was placed in India for governance and to report back to the Empire. **The first Governor General** was installed in **1772 - Warren Hastings.** He was a very skilful politician but his use of force and his greed led to his impeachment on charges of corruption!

It was not as if the British expansion proceeded unheeded. Several Rajas and Kings opposed the rapid rise of the British. One of the most famous was the Nawab of Mysore, **Tipu Sultan.** The British regarded him a dangerous foe and **killed him** in the **battle of Seringapatnam** in **1799.**

By the middle of the 1800's the whole of India came under British rule. In some places, though they did not govern the people directly, they installed friendly princes and Kings. Soon resentment began to rise among the people at the high-handed ways of the British. The foremost and the most memorable revolt was the Sepoy Mutiny.

Did you know that in **1876 Queen Victoria** took the title of **'Empress of India'?** The British holdings in India were now so large that the queen claimed the title of Empress and made the Governor General a Viceroy who would rule under her. The British viceroy enjoyed great personal power and prestige!

In 1885 the **Indian National Congress** was the founded by a liberal Englishman, A.O. Hume? At first the Congress was only a moderate body asking for reforms, but soon a stronger group emerged under the leadership of Bal Gangadhar Tilak from Maharashtra, Bipin Chandra Pal from Bengal and Lala Lajpat Rai from Punjab. They raised their voices and mobilised the people against the British.

The freedom struggle

As the British power rose and spread, another tide rose too. The tide of nationalism! Several educated Indians began to raise their voices against the might of the British Empire. They highlighted the drain of wealth and resources from India to Britain and asked for the British to use the democratic principles, that were being used all over the world, in India too.

Mohandas Karamchand Gandhi, the father of our nation and the true leader of the freedom struggle in India, joined the congress in 1915. The basis of Gandhiji's fight against the British was non-violence. He launched countrywide agitations against the British, in which not a man raised a hand or a weapon.

In 1942, Gandhi along with Jawaharlal Nehru launched the **Quit India Movement.** This non-violent stir against the British saw mass agitations. All leaders were arrested and this stir caused the world to wake up. The British had to begin talks with the Indian leaders and freedom was not far away for the Indians!

In August 1947, the struggle ended. The country was divided into India and Pakistan and was granted **independence** on the **15th of August, 1947.** Pakistan became an independent state a day earlier - 14th August 1947. **Jawaharlal Nehru,** the **first Prime Minister of free India** took over from **Lord Mount-batten** - the **last Governor General of British India.**

The great leaders of India

The father of our nation Mohandas Karamchand Gandhi was born in 1869. Leading the national struggle for freedom from the front, this courageous man, used non-violence and truth to shake the mighty British Empire in India. Gandhi was shot dead in January 1948. Did you know what the great scientist Albert Einstein said of Gandhi: "Generations to come will scarcely believe that such a one as this walked the earth in flesh and blood."

Jawaharlal Nehru was born in 1889. Though much younger than Gandhi, Nehru was a leader of great qualities and spirit. As the first Prime Minister of independent India, he shaped the country's destiny like no other man. He laid emphasis on industrialisation and gave importance to growth and development.

Sardar Vallabhbhai Patel was called the **Ironman of India.** He was a very strong leader who after independence brought in all the princely states under one sovereign and established the Republic of India. Patel's leadership qualities were matched only by his diplomatic skill!

Indira Gandhi, the daughter of Jawaharlal Nehru, not only participated in the freedom struggle in an active manner, but also became the first woman Prime Minister of India. Becoming Prime Minister in 1966, she guided the country on the road to progress, prosperity and recognition. She was assassinated in 1984.

Bhimrao Ramji Ambedkar was a social reformer and a great leader. Despite coming from a backward background, Ambedkar gained doctorates from Columbia University in New York City and the University of London. Ambedkar also was one of the key figures who wrote out the constitution of India. Ambedkar was honoured with the Bharat Ratna, India's highest civilian decoration.

The symbols of India

India's **national flag** is a tricolour of deep saffron, white and dark green, with the Dharma Chakra in the center of the white band. The saffron in the flag stands for courage, sacrifice and the spirit of renunciation; the white, for purity and truth; the green for faith and fertility. The chakra is the wheel of law that is found on the Sarnath Lion capital, too! This Buddhist symbol dates back to 200 B.C.

India's **national anthem,** Jana gana mana, was composed in Bengali by Rabindranath Tagore, the Nobel laureate. A beautifully rendered song, which starts off with the words that mean - Thou are the ruler of the minds of all people, dispenser of India's destiny - this anthem was first sung at the Calcutta session of the Indian National Congress on December 27th, 1911 and was adopted as the National Anthem of India on 24th January, 1950 by the Constituent Assembly.

Did you know that the Lotus is India's **national flower?** Regarded as a symbol of divinity and grace, this flower symbolizes purity, beauty, majesty, grace, fertility, wealth, richness, knowledge and serenity! And what about the **national tree** and the **national fruit?** The Banyan and the Mango! Now chew on that!

India's **national emblem** is a replica of the Lion of Sarnath. This lion capital, which was erected by Emperor Ashoka in the 3rd Century B.C. was the symbol of peace and Ashoka's renunciation of evil, warring ways. Today the national emblem serves to remind all of India's peaceful ways.

India's **national animals** are the Tiger and the Peacock. The tiger was chosen as a perfect symbol of grace, strength and power.
The Peacock was chosen because it stands for many a metaphor in almost all religions and is a perfect picture of secularism.

People of India, languages, cultures, food, religions, festivals...

With over 28 states and 7 Union Territories, India is a diverse country. As I told you before, there are 14 major and over a 1000 minor languages in India. Did you know that India's schools teach 58 different languages, and that there are newspapers in 87 languages, radio programmes in 71 and films in 15?

Films are a major source of entertainment for the public. In fact, the Indian film industry is regarded as the largest film industry in the world, in terms of the number of films produced every year. Film stars are considered gods in this film-crazy nation and there are some film stars who have had temples built for them!

India is a diverse land where a **festival** is celebrated almost every week. Each festival has its own significance, a legendary tale, a special way to celebrate it and also its own cuisine! Indians celebrate Pongal, the festival of harvest, Diwali, the festival of lights, Holi, the festival of colour, Christmas, Easter, Ramzan, Baisakhi and many others with equal gusto!

Did you know that the most popular sport in the country is **cricket?** If there's one thing that runs through the blood of all Indians it's the love of cricket.

The country's **cuisine** is a lip-smacking array from the heavily spiced food of the North to the light coconutty flavours of the South... from the fragrant meals of the east to the heady cuisine of the West. In fact each community has a special cuisine of their own, yummm! You've got to try it!

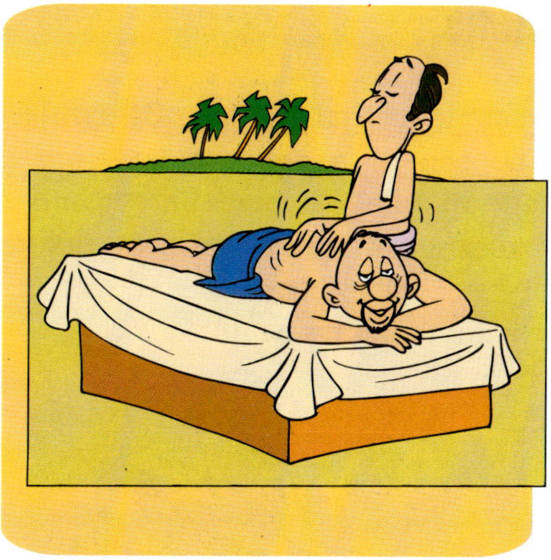

Places of travel

In fact, India offers the best travel and holiday experiences. Adventure tours, cultural tours, wildlife tours, Ayurveda & spa tours, festival tours… you can get them all. Or you can choose to view India's great heritage by visiting forts, palaces, monuments, temples… See the wildlife and experience the beauty of the land by going on Elephant safari tours, wildlife parks and sanctuaries… India has them all!

Some of the most exciting tours are the **Tiger Tours** of India. I went through all the national parks and reserves in India, right from the Corbett National Park to some of the smaller parks and saw the beautiful animals in majestic repose! Would you like to try that out?

Another exciting tour to take is the **Temple Tour**. Do you know that I visited all the major temples in North as well as South India? The best thing about temple tours is to be able to walk through the temple cities.

If you would like something to keep, then do take an art and craft tour through India! You can go through all the old cities and places, like exciting Rajasthan, vibrant Gujarat, old-worldly Tamil Nadu, calm Kerala… and pick up some of the most beautiful and exquisitely made regional handicrafts…

But top of the list has got to be Kerala… situated in the southernmost part of the country; this tiny region offers the greenest and the calmest holiday ever! A journey through Kerala is a holiday for the mind, body and soul! I have promised to take Professor Janus there, next year. Would you like to join us?

Great Indians

Jehangir Ratanji Dadabhoy Tata, was the doyen of Indian industry and a pioneering aviator. He headed one of the largest industrial empires in the country, Tata Sons, for over five decades. He qualified as India's first pilot and founded Tata Airlines, which later became the country's national flier, Air India.

Another great industrialist was **Dhirubhai Ambani!** The son of a petty trader from a remote village in rural Gujarat, he became a billionaire industrialist, with a business empire built on polyester. Dhirubhai's dream was the creation of wealth for all his people, for which he was much loved and admired.

Born August 26, 1910, in Skopje, **Agnes Gonxha Bojaxhiu** was the daughter of Albanian parents. At the age of 18, she was inspired to work in India and joined a community of Irish nuns with a mission in Calcutta, taking the name of **Sister Teresa.** She spent 17 years teaching and 50 years in the service of Calcutta's poor, who saw in her the face of God!

Some top sportsmen have brought honour and glory to India. **Geet Sethi** has won the Billiards World Championship an amazing 6 times. **Viswanathan Anand** has been the FIDE World Chess Champion! **Sachin Tendulkar,** considered by many to be the greatest cricketer ever, has not only scored the highest number of runs in one-dayers, he has also made a record number of centuries in the limited overs version of the game.

A scientist president! **A. P. J. Abdul Kalam** is today India's first people's president, who takes every opportunity to reach out to people, especially children, whom he recognises as the hope of India. India's premier scientist and father of the country's defence programme, Kalam has been honoured with the Bharat Ratna, India's highest civilian award!

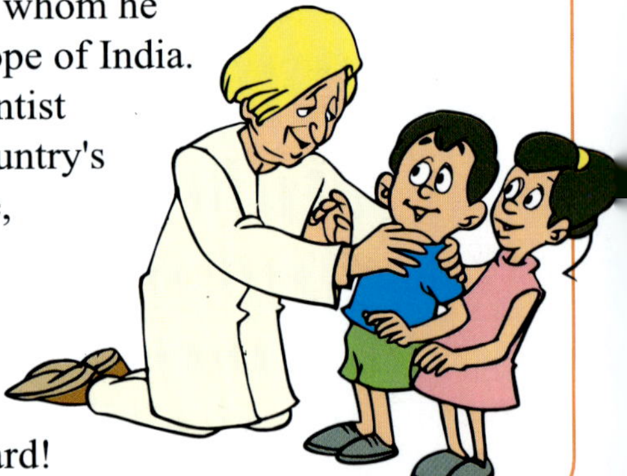